Hon...., __

Penny Roker RSM is a Sister of Mercy, a religious order with members worldwide. Her own Community is in Peterborough where the Sisters lead day retreats and prayer workshops. She also works as a prison chaplain and has used these meditations in both spheres of her ministry.

For my parents

HOMELY LOVE

*Prayers and reflections
using the words of
Julian of Norwich*

Sr Penny Roker RSM

CANTERBURY
PRESS
Norwich

First published in 2006 by the Canterbury Press Norwich
(a publishing imprint of Hymns Ancient & Modern Limited,
a registered charity)
13–17 Long Lane, London ECIA 9PN

www.scm-canterburypress.co.uk

Second impression 2010

Bible quotations are taken from The New Jerusalem Bible,
published and copyright © 1966, 1967 and 1968 by Darton,
Longman and Todd Ltd and Doubleday, a division of
Random House, Inc. and used by permission.

British Library Cataloguing in Publication data

A catalogue record for this book is available
from the British Library

ISBN 978 1 85311 733 6

Typeset by Regent Typesetting, London
Printed and bound by
CPI Antony Rowe, Chippenham, Wiltshire

Contents

I am especially grateful to Sr Pamela CAH, Guest
Sister of All Hallows next to the Julian Shrine,
for her enthusiasm and very helpful revisions.
I would also like to thank Sr Chris Bendin RSM,
my own Community, and the Leadership Team
of the Institute of Our Lady of Mercy for the
encouragement they have given to this book.

Introduction

The reputation of Julian of Norwich as a mystic and a spiritual writer, already established in her own lifetime 600 years ago, has never stood higher than it does today. Our generation has paused in its frantic consumerism to consider what may expand the soul in proportion to the mind and body. We seem never to tire of what Julian has to say.

People have not always, however, felt comfortable with every aspect of her thinking. Jesus, she tells us, is our Mother. In God, she insists, there is no anger. It is all the more fascinating that challenging ideas of this kind should have come from a medieval woman.

Curiosity is also aroused by Julian's situation as an anchoress. For modern people, shocked by the experience of terrorist hostages like Terry Waite, solitary confinement has dreadful associations. For a young woman of only 30 to embrace the life of a recluse voluntarily seems incomprehensible. Yet in the Middle Ages a steady number of people, monks and nuns as well as ordinary men and women, sought greater seclusion in order to devote themselves to prayer and contemplation. Towns were proud of their 'recluses'. They welcomed the spiritual and material blessings such holy people were likely to bring to the community as a whole.

Unlike hermits, who were not walled in and often lived a wandering life, anchorites and their female equivalent, anchoresses, were enclosed in a room or rooms (their 'anchorage') by a church, never to leave. This radical lifestyle was not lightly undertaken. Such a calling required careful discernment. Church authorities needed to be sure that the individual had a true vocation and the necessary inner and material resources. For an anchorite to go mad or to die of neglect would not have served anyone's interests. The ceremony of enclosure reflected the seriousness of the step they were undertaking. In a solemn rite the anchorite professed their vows and then entered the cell in procession with priests and attendants. The cell was blessed. Then came the dramatic moment. When all but the anchorite had withdrawn, the wall was blocked up. It must have felt like being buried alive.

This did not, in reality, mean utter isolation. There was access for visitors and servants. Julian, we know, had two servants, Alice and Sara. She also had a cat. Her cell had a window into the church through which she could take part in services. Another window looked out onto St Julian's Alley which ran down to the River Wensum nearby. No doubt a stream of passers-by brought noise and chatter, news and greetings throughout the day. We know of at least one celebrated visitor who came specifically to see Julian – this was Margery Kempe from King's Lynn, herself a spiritual writer, who carefully documented their conversation. Julian cannot be accused of cutting herself off from real life. In her writings she was ever aware of her fellow human beings, or 'even Christians' as she called them.

The Church of St Julian still stands, though it was bombed in the war. Julian's cell had to be rebuilt. Its present floor level is lower than it would have been in Julian's day, so she would have felt much more a part of parish life than the present high window into the church might suggest. As in her own day, a constant stream of visitors from far and near continues to seek the sanctuary of this place.

Little is known about Julian's personal background. The date of her birth is likely to have been late 1342 since she describes her visionary experience as having occurred in May 1373 at the age of thirty-and-a-half. There is documentary evidence that she was still alive into at least her seventies. She was variously described as Dame, Lady and Mother Julian. What this may indicate about her social and religious status is still hotly debated. We do not know whether she was a nun; whether she was widowed or had children; whether she was educated, well connected, or poor. What we can be confident about is that her near-death experience during the night of 8 May 1373 changed her life. She devoted the rest of it to contemplation of all that she had experienced of Christ's love, and recorded it in a book called *Showing of Love*. These visions nourished her for a lifetime. She hoped that they might nourish us too.

Much of Julian of Norwich's book is more to medieval than to modern taste. The sixteen 'shewings' or revelations focus on the sufferings of Christ in graphic detail. This was the emphasis of devotional works at the time. But there are other rich dimensions to Julian's writings, as countless readers have discovered over the centuries.

Julian produced more than one version of her revelations, leaving us with a rich composite. There is, as a backbone, the description of her revelations of Christ's Passion which she saw with her 'bodily eye'. To fill out this eyewitness account of her deathbed visions, there is additional spiritual insight from her own ponderings over the years that followed. Interspersed are homely examples which she draws from her everyday experience to make sense of it all. The focus of this book is on these 'homely touches', glimpses of Julian's own domestic routine, of medieval life, of human preoccupations which are the same now as in her day 600 years ago – gardening, clothes, medicine, floor-tiles and the like. Each chapter takes one of these as its theme.

There are six clear sections to each chapter, beginning with a passage 'From Julian's Writings'. This is followed by a reflection which places the passage in its historical, domestic and spiritual context. 'Sharing Julian's Experience' invites the reader to reflect on their own personal experience. A biblical passage is provided 'For Further Reflection' – Julian's own reflections were steeped in familiar passages of Scripture, which she knew and loved. The reading and reflection may give rise to spontaneous prayer. For those who prefer to use the words and inspiration of Julian herself, the next section is simply called 'Prayer'. Each chapter is brought to a close by a prayer or blessing called 'Endings'.

The individual reader might consider setting aside an hour or so to work with each chapter as a whole. This approach would suit groups who have a block of time available for prayer workshops or retreat days. Some people might prefer just to dip in here and there, especially if they only have a few minutes to spare for quiet time each day. The separate passages, prayers and exercises can easily stand alone for this or for liturgical use. Complete services of Morning and of Evening Prayer are also included.

My purpose in assembling this book is to enable people to access and to apply the spiritual riches of Julian with no resources other than those to be found around the house. Organized retreats can be expensive, and people may not be able to afford either the holiday time or the money. Those who have most time for reflection, such as prisoners, the housebound and elderly people, are least likely to be able to take up opportunities offered by churches and retreat centres. They often have to 'make do' spiritually. I hope this may help.

This 'homely' approach would, I think, meet with Julian's approval. Julian herself stayed right where she was in her home city and sought contemplative stillness in an anchorage adjoining a Norwich parish church. There she was sought out for her advice and counselling. She may even have felt pestered at times. We know that she had domestic help. So Julian's spirituality was not entirely removed from human society or from the pressures and concerns of ordinary everyday life.

For Julian, as for my own Community of Sisters of Mercy, the cloister is wherever need or circumstance find us. Our Foundress, Catherine McAuley, practical to the last, suggested from her deathbed that her Sisters should gather for a 'comfortable cup of tea'. Her letters convey the same human touch that we see and love in the writings of Julian: humour, common sense and compassion for people in the situations they find themselves in.

This book, then, might be an armchair retreat for those whose spiritual input must be found for the most part in the ordinariness of home life. As Julian herself came to understand,

> This is how it is with our Lord Jesus and us, for surely it is the greatest joy possible, as I see it, that he who is highest and mightiest, noblest and worthiest, is . . . homeliest and most friendly.

I

The Curate's Crucifix

Astonished by God

And I said: Hello, Lord!

FROM JULIAN'S WRITINGS

After this my sight began to fail and it was all dark about me in the chamber as if it were night except for the image of the cross, within which I saw a kind of light, I didn't know how . . .

All of a sudden I saw red blood trickling down from under the crown of thorns . . . And I said:
                    Hello, Lord!

This I said at the top of my voice, though I meant it reverently, completely astonished as I was and taken aback that he that is so holy and awesome would want to be so homely with a sinful creature living in wretched flesh . . .

And as long as I saw this sight of the plenteous bleeding of the head, I never stopped saying these words: 'Welcome, Lord!' . . . (3, 4, 8)

On 8 May (or possibly the 13th) 1373, Julian lay dying. She was only 30 years old. We don't know what the illness was, but for days she lingered close to death. She had lost all feeling from the waist down and lay waiting to die. She asked to be helped to sit up to breathe her last. By the time the curate arrived to give the last rites, her eyes were already fixed and she had lost the power of speech. He held the crucifix before her face and told her to comfort herself with the image of her Maker and Saviour. At this, her sight began to fail and the room darkened except for a light coming from within the crucifix. All around seemed ugly, she said, as if occupied by something evil. All feeling began to ebb away.

Unlike today, where anointing is for the sick, not just a last rite for the dying, the arrival of the priest was feared in medieval times. It was his duty to ensure that the dying person repented and had complete trust in Christ, and so people expected the devil to be especially active around the bedside. The Church in those days anointed only sick persons whose death was imminent. That must have felt like a certain death sentence. It was commonly believed that, even if you recovered, you could never live normally again. For, however much people were reassured to the contrary, anointing was seen as consecration, obliging the person to remain celibate for the rest of their days. This may explain Julian's choice of lifestyle after her recovery.

For Julian, the experience had an unexpected twist. After the priest's visit there was a sudden change, all pain went, and Julian felt fit and whole. Unexpectedly, from the crucifix, she began to see red blood appearing from under the crown of thorns, hot and fresh and plentiful. She realized that this was a revelation to her from God himself. And so, instead of the usual deathbed terrors, her heart was filled with astonished joy. Her bedside companions must have been equally astonished, for she suddenly called out,

'Hello, Lord!' Her exact words were, 'Benedicite Domine!' or 'Bless you, Lord!' which sounds very formal. But 'Benedicite!' was a traditional way for nuns to greet each other, so it was more like saying 'Hello' or 'Welcome' in a friendly sort of way. She was completely taken aback that God himself had visited her in this homely manner while she lay propped up on the pillows.

In all Julian received sixteen 'shewings' or revelations. A number of them were visions of Christ's passion, the sufferings he underwent on the cross. But it is by no means a gloomy or frightening sequence. Her intention was for the reader to experience the same intense joy and comfort that Julian herself derived from the revelation of God's love for his people. The message throughout the visions is of God's goodness and of his loving delight in all that he has created.

That day altered the course of her life. For 20 years Julian reflected on the visions she received in those few hours. In her book, which she called *Showing of Love*, she invites us to share them with her.

SHARING JULIAN'S EXPERIENCE

Set up a crucifix before you
and a lighted candle.
A spotlight might help.

Sit still for a while before the crucifix.
Looking at this image of Jesus can arouse mixed feelings:
horror, guilt, thankfulness, compassion, love, obligation

. . .

and yet Julian's feeling was of astonishment!

Homely Love

So think back to a time when you have been astonished
by something you weren't expecting to happen,
something that 'lit up' a situation in a delightful or new
  way.
Look at what it was that thrilled you.

  Did it change the way you saw yourself?

  Did you feel more lovable, perhaps, than you thought?

  Did you feel more cared for than you dared hope?

As you recall the feeling, look at the image of your
  Saviour and Maker.
Say, as Julian did,

  Benedicite Domine!
  or Hello, Lord!
  or Welcome, Life!

Use any homely words of greeting that you feel
  comfortable with.
You might try addressing God in a way you are not used
  to doing.

In the evening of that same day, the first day of the week, the doors were closed in the room where the disciples were, for fear of the Jews. Jesus came and stood among them. He said to them, 'Peace be with you,' and, after saying this, he showed them his hands and his side. The disciples were filled with joy at seeing the Lord, and he said to them again,

'Peace be with you.'

John 20. 19–21

PRAYER

The 'Benedicite Prayer'

I kept saying these words, Welcome Lord!

This prayer uses Julian's description of how it felt on her sickbed at the time she received the visions.

when all around seems ugly
you remind us of love
and we say, Welcome, Lord!

when we weary of living
you awake us with joy
and we say, Welcome, Lord!

when darkness closes round
you light us from within
and we say, Welcome, Lord!

when we are numb to feeling
you restore us to life
and we say, Welcome, Lord!

when we know only pain
you give us release
and we say, Welcome, Lord!

when we have no words
you're there in our silence
and we say, Welcome, Lord!

when our eyes cannot see
you astonish us with presence
and we say, Welcome, Lord!

ENDINGS

The Trinity Prayer (44)

Julian refers often to the Holy Trinity. The medieval Cathedral of Norwich, which she would have known well, was dedicated to the Holy and Undivided Trinity.

may Wisdom make me certain

Wisdom gazes on God

you are Wisdom

May Truth make it clear

Truth sees God

You are Truth

Lord,

you are Love

Love delights in God

that I am made for Love

made for Love

2

The Lesson

Loved by God

He wants us to have some knowledge here of our A B C. (80)

FROM JULIAN'S WRITINGS

... our soul is so specially loved by God Most High that it surpasses the knowledge of any creature – that is to say, there is no created being can understand how much and how sweetly and how tenderly our Maker loves us ... And therefore we may ask of our Lover with reverence all that we desire, for our natural will is to have God and the good will of God is to have us. And we will never cease wanting nor longing until we have him in fullness of joy, and then we shall want no more. For he wills that we should live in that knowledge and love until that time when we are fulfilled in heaven. And therefore was this lesson of love shown. (6)

'What is wrong with my prayer life?' we sometimes wonder. We seem to end up just pleading for things without much real hope of an answer. Julian recognized this. It is, she said, because we haven't learned the 'lesson of love'. Julian said that the Showings were given to her because of our 'lack of understanding and knowledge of love', and in chapter 6 she invites us to understand something of the love of God,

    that he loves you, for you are the soul he has made in
      his own likeness;

    that he does not despise you, for you are the work of his
      hands;

    that he delights to serve you, however petty your needs
      might seem.

Above all, your eternal lover longs for you to cling to
him. When we come to realize this, then we will have con-
fidence that all we need will be provided. With the realiza-
tion of God's deep love for us, every other concern will
start to fall into place. This is the 'lesson of love' Julian was
given: simply that God loves us. When we bring our needs
before God in prayer, it can be in the knowledge and 'full
security' of being loved.

It took Julian a long time to understand this lesson. She
received the Showings in 1373 and prayed to know their
meaning. It was 15 years or more before she received, or
perhaps until she absorbed, her answer. That answer she
describes in chapter 86: 'Thus was I learned that love was
his meaning.' She called her book *Showing of Love*. As far
as Julian was concerned, the 16 visions were simply one
and the same: the revealing of God's love for us.

Her final chapter acknowledges that the lesson is not yet
fully learned. We need, she says, to pray to God for the
grace to love and to cling to him. Our prayer life grows
when our hearts are 'thanking, trusting, enjoying' God,
when it reflects a sense of relatedness to him. Prayer is more
than just words: it flows from our centredness in him. As
God said 'full merrily' to Julian, 'I am the ground of your
beseeching'.

As Julian explains, before God made us he loved us, and
that love has never lessened. It shall never tire out in any

way nor go sour nor become outgrown nor be superseded as some human loves can be when someone new comes along. It is this ever-new and enduring love which motivates each act of creation. It is in this love that God has purposed everything that happens to us to be in some way for our good, even if we cannot understand how. And it is in this loving embrace that our life goes on forever.

In our making we had beginning,
but the love with which he made us was in him without beginning,
and in that love we have our beginning.
And all this shall be seen in God without end.
This may Jesus grant us.
Amen. (86)

SHARING JULIAN'S EXPERIENCE

Write *a b c* in large letters with your left hand on a piece of paper
or with your right hand if you are left-handed.

Sit quietly with the letters.
Recall how difficult it is to begin or to re-learn anything

such as your first steps after an illness,
or a foreign language,
or having driving lessons.

Time and the effort of trying are required.
Eventually there comes understanding and ease.
The same may be true of loving.

How loving am I?
Julian offers two clues.

She says God's kind of love

   'brings life' to a soul

   and 'makes it grow'. (6)

Think of the people who are important to you.
   Have you/they found the relationship life-giving?
   Have you/they found the relationship growthful?

FOR FURTHER REFLECTION

We have recognized for ourselves, and put our faith
in, the love God has for us. God is love, and whoever
remains in love remains in God and God in him. Love
comes to its perfection in us when we can face the Day of
Judgement fearlessly, because even in this world we have
become as he is. In love there is no room for fear, but per-
fect love drives out fear, because fear implies punishment
and no one who is afraid has come to perfection in love.
Let us love, then, because he first loved us.

1 John 4. 16–19

Homely Love

PRAYER

*Understanding and knowing that he is all goodness is the highest prayer
and it comes down to the lowest part of our need. (6)*

Lord,

I bring you the lowest part of my need;
I bring you the deepest part of myself.
Help me understand what love is,
and to know it in my life.
May learning how to love
bring life and growth
to myself and others.
And may this life of love
be true worship
of you who first loved us.

Amen.

ENDINGS

Julian asked God for the meaning behind the 'Showings'.
Fifteen years later he answered:

Do you want to know your Lord's meaning in this thing?
Know this well: Love was his meaning.
Who showed it to you? Love.
What did he show you? Love.
Why did he show you? For Love.
Hold on to this. (86)

Lord, I want to know the meaning
behind my life's experiences.
Help me know that love gives them meaning.
Who shows me this? Love.
What are you showing me? Love.
Why do you show me? For Love.
Help me to hold on to this too.

3

The Guest

At Home with God

*Almost forgetting himself for joy
at this great homeliness* (7)

It is the greatest honour that a solemn king or a great lord may do to a
poor servant if he is willing to be homely with him ... Then this poor
creature thinks,

'Ah! What greater respect and joy could this noble lord give me than
to show a simple person like me such marvellous homeliness? Truly,
it is more joy and delight to me than if he gave me great gifts and were
distant in his manner ...'

This is how it is with our Lord Jesus and us, for surely it is the greatest
joy possible, as I see it, that he who is highest and mightiest, noblest and
worthiest, is lowest and meekest, homeliest and most friendly. (7)

Julian lived in a society of strict social conventions. Class
division was not just a question of rich and poor as it is in
the West today. In those days the gulf was wider. Wealth
alone would not make a lady or gentleman of you. Laws
regarding codes of dress preserved distinctions between

noble and commoner. French was the language of the court; Latin the language of academics, lawyers and churchmen; and English the language of working people. Social barriers extended even to the Church where noble families dominated the higher clergy and where even religious orders were divided into 'choir' and 'lay' monks and nuns according to social status.

The monks of Norwich Cathedral and the nuns of Carrow Priory, to which St Julian's church and its anchorage belonged, were both Benedictine communities. We do not know whether Julian herself was ever professed as a nun. Her mother's attendance at her sick-bed suggests that, at least at that time, she was not. We do not know what her social status was at all. Though her writings suggest that she was widely read, she describes herself as 'a simple creature that could no letter'. Her language is English and down to earth. It may be that she was marginalized in some way – aspiring to religious life but unqualified; disabled perhaps and unmarried; maybe withdrawing from society after receiving the last rites of the Church; or widowed and bereaved of her children after the ravages of the Black Death that struck three times in her lifetime in 1349, 1362 and 1369. We may never know her circumstances of life.

What we do know of Julian is something of her depth of feeling at the condescension of God in making himself at home with a simple creature. I like to think that this meant so much to her because Julian knew what it was to be snubbed or passed over by those who thought themselves to be above her. She talks about 'some great lord' as if nobility was something she had experienced only from an admiring distance.

Perhaps in childhood she had been dazzled by the passing of some sumptuously dressed lords and ladies and daydreamed that one would stoop down to befriend her. How many of us have fantasized that someone rich and famous, a pop star or football celebrity or someone royal, would meet us by chance and become a personal friend? For Julian this became a living reality when the crucifix set before her eyes brought Christ in an unimaginably real way to her bedside. The living presence of Jesus remained with her and transformed her life.

The living presence of Jesus in Word, in sacrament, and in our brothers and sisters remains with us too. His Spirit is with us. Whatever lack of status we may have felt or experienced, it is a source of wonderment and joy that the Lord of all creation knocks at our door and makes himself at home. The question is, how welcome do we make this honoured guest?

SHARING JULIAN'S EXPERIENCE

Put on your slippers or bedsocks
or do whatever you need to feel really at home.

What does 'homely' mean for you?

Imagine Christ being homely with you.

Julian wrote:

> Our Lord God showed that it is full great pleasure to him
> that a silly soul come to him nakedly and plainly and homely. (5)

By 'silly', Julian meant 'simple' in the sense of unaffected.

She means that you can be yourself in God's presence,

nakedly, that is, without defences

plainly, that is, without any special way of speaking

homely, that is, just as you are.

FOR FURTHER REFLECTION

Look, I am standing at the door, knocking. If one of you hears me calling and opens the door, I will come in to share a meal at that person's side. Anyone who proves victorious I will allow to share my throne, just as I have myself overcome and have taken my seat with my father on his throne.

Revelation 3. 20–21

PRAYER

The 'Lo me' Prayer

Lo me, God's handmaid. (4)

These are the words Julian uses to describe Mary's response at the Annunciation.
In modern language it is usually translated as 'Behold the handmaid of the Lord'.

A little boy I know begins his prayers in similar fashion: 'This is me, Kieran'.

Homely Love

This is me, Lord,
the door is open.
I want my heart
to be open too.

This is me, Lord,
the hearth is waiting.
I still my mind
to wait for you.

ENDINGS

God, of your goodness,
give me yourself,
for you are enough for me
and, to give you due honour,
I cannot ask for less.
And were I to ask anything less,
I should always want more.
In you alone do I have everything. (5)

4

Our Clothes

Hugged by God

How God is to us everything that is good,
tenderly wrapping us. (5)

FROM JULIAN'S WRITINGS

Our Lord showed to me a spiritual insight of his homely loving. I saw that he is everything that is good and comfortable for us. He is our clothing that for love wraps us, hugs us and, out of tender love, completely encloses us, never to leave us . . .

. . . for as the body is clad in the cloth . . . so are we, soul and body, clad in the goodness of God and enclosed; yea, and more homely still, for these may waste and wear away, [but] the goodness of God remains whole and even closer to us . . . there is no creature that is made that may know how much and how sweetly and how tenderly our maker loves us. (5–6)

Clothes say a lot about who we are and how we feel about ourselves. Though we would be foolish to try to sum up anyone just by their physical appearance, clothes can be an expression of our unique personalities. They may give a message about how we see ourselves or aspire to be. They may also reflect our mood, our relationship to the environment and sometimes our role in the community. Clothes are physically close to our bodies and can contribute to a sense of security or well-being.

One of Julian's 'shewings' was of a great lord and his servant. In chapter 51 of her book, she describes the lord as wearing ample folds of cloth in azure blue, while the servant was clad simply as a working man. She gives every detail of his old defaced tunic, un-dyed except for being stained with sweat, tight-fitting because he had grown out of it, short above the knee, and almost worn out.

From her description – and you can almost see her turning her nose up in disgust – she seemed to know full well what old clothes looked and smelled like. Perhaps she herself had to wear them. They symbolized the frailty, poverty and life of labour common to many of us. And yet, however unattractive some clothes might be, Julian uses such clothing as a picture of the intimacy with which God loves us, protecting, enfolding and holding us close. Julian's reaction to the vision of the poorly clad servant was to exclaim with surprise:

'Now this is unseemly clothing for a servant that is so greatly loved to appear in before so honoured a lord!' But within him I could see a deep love, a love he felt towards the lord which was like the love the lord had for him. (51)

When we contemplate this deep relationship between ourselves and God, a love which goes far beyond our external circumstances or appearance, we can begin to accept ourselves. It does not matter how beautiful or disfigured we are; how elegant or un-presentable; how bulky or athletic; how easygoing or awkward. All that really matters is that God loves us just as we are.

Secure in that love, we can become less self-absorbed and fretful, and develop the capacity to become more outward-looking, accepting and compassionate to others:

> And this is why the lesson of love was shown . . . seeing the loving of its maker makes the soul seem less import-ant in its own sight and fills it up with reverend fear and true meekness with plenty of Christian love for its fellow men. (6)

The 'true meekness' Julian speaks of is not false modesty, but being unselfconsciously 'just as we are'. This is the kind of poverty of spirit Jesus spoke of: not full of myself, but content to be as I am made; not putting myself down, but recognizing my dependence upon God for all that I need.

SHARING JULIAN'S EXPERIENCE

Find a favourite garment or shoes.
It must be your own.

To ponder:

What is it that you like about it?

How do you feel when you put it on?

What might it bring to mind about God's love for you?

For example,

I chose this jacket because I like its colour. I feel brighter
when I put it on. It makes me think of the way God
gives me energy for life.

These are my old slippers. They're worn to my shape and
I feel comfortable and more 'myself' when I wear them.
It helps me understand that God accepts me just as I
am.

This is my favourite skirt. The pleats stay in shape. I
feel smart in it. This is how God loves me: he always
sees the best in me even when other people criticize.

FOR FURTHER REFLECTION

Jerusalem, take off your dress of sorrow and distress,
put on the beauty of God's glory for evermore, wrap the
cloak of God's saving justice around you, put the diadem
of the Eternal One's glory on your head, for God means
to show your splendour to every nation under heaven,
and the name God gives you for evermore will be, 'Peace-
through-Justice, and Glory-through-Devotion'.

Baruch 5. 1–4

Our Clothes

There have been times when I have felt shown up and humiliated.
Lord, when I am naked before others, be . . .

my clothing that wraps me in love.

There have been times when I have felt left out and rejected.
Lord, when I am neglected by others, be . . .

my clothing that hugs me in love.

There have been times when I have felt unprotected and let down.
Lord, when I am vulnerable to others, be . . .

my clothing that completely closes me round
in tender love, never to leave me.

And for all the times when you gave me such love,

I thank you, Lord,
for as the body is clad in the cloth,
and the flesh in the skin,
and the bones in the flesh,
and the heart in the trunk,
so am I, soul and body,
wrapped round in your favour.
Amen.

                                        (5–6 adapted)

Homely Love

Bless you, Lord.
Bless Jesus, God-and-Man,
our everlasting joy and bliss.
Bless God the Trinity,
our Maker, our Keeper, our Lover.
Bless you, Lord.

(4 adapted)

5

The Hazelnut

Resting in God

For this is the reason why we are not completely at ease in our heart and soul, for here we seek rest in these things that are so little in which there is no rest and do not know our God. (5)

FROM JULIAN'S WRITINGS

He showed me more, a little thing, the size of a hazel nut in the palm of my hand, and it was as round as a ball. I looked upon it with the eye of my understanding and thought, 'What may this be?' And it was answered in this way, 'It is all that is made.' I marvelled how it might last, for I thought to myself it might suddenly disintegrate it was so little. And I came to an understanding: it lasts and always shall, because God loves it, and so all things have their being because of the love of God. In this little thing I saw three truths: the first is that God made it, the second is that God loves it, the third is that God keeps it. (5)

In contemplating creation in all its wonder, diversity, intricacy and beauty, we are sometimes touched by a deep sense of relatedness to the world around. It draws us beyond ourselves. God reveals himself to us in his creation and we acknowledge and thank God as our maker and as the source of life and love. It is in right relationship with God, with ourselves, with other people and with the earth that we find peace and meaning to life.

But engagement with the world around us can also make us vulnerable. Loving and living to the full open us up to hurt and disappointment as well as to delight and fulfilment. As Julian says of Mary, the mother of Jesus, who was fully involved with her Son's mission, 'the greatness of his loving was the cause of the greatness of her pain' (18). After all, it led him to the cross. It is tempting to limit our involvement with others in order to insure ourselves against every kind of emotional and material loss and injury. Yet Christ was willing to take the risk of making himself vulnerable by his loving involvement with the life of the creation.

The hazelnut of Julian's vision seems to symbolize this created world of people and things. This world looms large for many of us. We may become anxious, insecure, guilty, competitive and grasping because of it. Our relationship to it is often based on fear, not love. Whether we are afraid *for* it or afraid *of* it, the image of the hazelnut reassures us. For those who see everything and everybody as fragile and in danger of being lost or hurt, Julian says its littleness is safe in God's love: 'it lasts and always will for God loves it'. For those who fear people and situations as threatening to themselves, Julian says creation, for all its majesty, amounts to very little when seen in the perspective of God's eternal power: like the hazelnut 'it is all that is made'.

Julian recognized that a human soul, created in love by God and for God, can never know complete rest or joy until it is so united to God that there is absolutely nothing 'betwixt my God and me'. She was not suggesting a cold-hearted spirituality detached from the material world.

After all, Christ was flesh and blood, at home in the crowd, among the fishing nets, cooking breakfast on the beach, eating out with friends. He felt grief for Lazarus, fear for his own life, anger at his disciples, and a special closeness to certain people. But it was the creator he worshipped, not the creation.

In aspiring to union with God, Julian does not encourage us to turn our backs on our friends and loved ones, nor to care any less for our environment, but to develop a sense of perspective in which all things are God's. We have to understand the 'littlehood of creatures' and to diminish the sway over us which people and situations and things can sometimes have. That includes our own needs. Spiritual 'rest' requires the bringing down in size and significance, Julian says, of the created world in our minds. She says they need to be 'noughted' – it is a wonderful old word. Next time a problem starts to get out of proportion, try using Julian's word and say, 'This needs noughting!'

SHARING JULIAN'S EXPERIENCE

Buy some hazelnuts.

Shelled ones from the health food store or supermarket are 'round like a ball' as Julian describes.

You might prefer to buy them with their shells still on and to crack them open as part of this prayerful exercise.
By damaging some you will demonstrate
what Julian was saying about the created world
when she said she was afraid
'that it might suddenly disintegrate it was so little'.

Homely Love

Ponder the hazelnut kernel in your hand
which represents the created world.

What is *your* 'world'?

Think about the important aspects of your life:

   family, friends, job, hobbies, worries, concerns,
   plans, dreams, prize possessions, health etc.

Look at the hazelnut and say to yourself:

'This is my world.
It is held in God's love.'

FOR FURTHER REFLECTION

After sending the crowds away he went up into the hills
by himself to pray. When evening came, he was there
alone, while the boat, by now some furlongs from land,
was hard pressed by rough waves, for there was a head-
wind. In the fourth watch of the night he came towards
them, walking on the sea, and when the disciples saw
him walking on the sea they were terrified. 'It is a ghost,'
they said, and cried out in fear. But at once Jesus called
out to them, saying, 'Courage! It's me! Don't be afraid.' It
was Peter who answered. 'Lord,' he said, 'if it is you, tell
me to come to you across the water.' Jesus said, 'Come.'
Then Peter got out of the boat and started walking towards Jesus across the water, but then noticing the wind,
he took fright and began to sink. 'Lord,' he cried, 'save
me!' Jesus put out his hand at once and held him.

Matthew 14. 23–31

The Hazelnut

The Hazelnut Mantra

Identify the aspects of your life, people, situations,
   things, which cause you concern or insecurity:

   your health, perhaps,
   or money,
   or a relationship.

As you name each one, gently close your fingers over the
   hazelnut, repeating Julian's words from chapter 5:

   God made it or him/her
   God loves it or him/her
   God keeps it or him/her

. . . then open your hand
and entrust it to God's care.

Say a definite 'Amen!' at the end as you leave it with him.

ENDINGS

Lord, your goodness enfolds all your creatures
and all your blessed works.
Your goodness goes on without end
for you are endlessness itself.

Homely Love

You have made us for yourself alone;
you have restored us by your blessed passion;
you keep us in your blessed love.

And all this is of your goodness.

Amen.

(5 adapted)

6

The Needle's Point

At One with God

For there is no doer but he. (11)

And after this I saw God in my mind's eye as a point, by which I saw that he is in all things. I reflected on what I beheld, troubled by the thought, 'What then is sin?' For I saw truly that God is behind everything, however little it might be. And I saw truly that nothing happens by accident or chance, but everything by God's wisdom which knows everything before it happens. If it seems to be by accident or chance in the eyes of man, then our blindness and our blinkeredness is the cause . . . for he is in the mid-point of all things and everything is his doing, and I was certain he commits no sin . . . our Lord wills to have the soul really turned to gaze on him and on all his works, for they are wholly good . . . There is no doer but he. I saw for certain that he never changes his purpose in any manner of thing, nor never shall; for from before the beginning there was nothing unknown to him without him ordaining it. (11)

Needlework was an important occupation in the days before sewing machines. There were clothes, hangings, linens and vestments to make up and to embellish by hand. Julian, like other women, had surely been taught to ply her

31

needle and still did so as an anchoress. As thread began to fill the cloth, she perhaps reflected on the canvas of time as it fills up with the deeds and dramas of human history. Other women no doubt chattered over their needlework, but Julian, solitary for much of her time, more than likely worked in silence.

I like to think of Julian in deep contemplation as she worked her needle. Perhaps it was then that she began to ponder the idea of God as a point. It seems strange to picture God mystically symbolized as a single point, but this is not intended to reduce God. On the contrary, a point symbolizes the very centre of all things. It is the unifying factor, with everything else in dependent relationship. A point has no substance or dimension: nor can God be measured or defined or grasped or divided. We can attempt to describe him by what he does and what he is like. We can, for example, say that he is a good shepherd, gathering in, protecting; or that he is a king, ruling and guiding; a father, loving and bringing into life. But his actual being is beyond description or understanding.

Julian does not use this symbol with the intention of making God strange to us. After all, her whole book is about God-with-us in Jesus. No, the image of God as a point at the centre of all that there is reassures us. It comforts us that nothing is beyond his reach or beyond his love, for he is in everything. Everything depends upon him. Nothing by sin or chance can fall out of his good purpose, for all things will come together for good, no matter how lost, fragmented or tainted they may seem to our limited human understanding. Nothing is hopeless.

If God made everything and is in everything, then the question of how sin came about presents a problem for

Julian as well as for many other people. Julian addresses the issue at length in her book, never quite able to answer the question completely other than to accept that, however it came about, God can bring good from it and that nothing is impossible to God in restoring his creation.

For at the centre of all things, God is. As Julian repeatedly says, he is 'without beginning' and 'without end', beyond time. What is past and future for us is all-present to the eternal Father. Our oneness with the God who is 'endlessness' itself (chapter 5) puts a different perspective on our regrets for what is done and our anxieties over what is yet to be. For neither we, nor what seems beyond us in time past or time to come, is ever beyond God's love or power.

SHARING JULIAN'S EXPERIENCE

Set up a piece of cloth with a needle stuck into the middle.

Picture the creative life force, the energy of love, coming from the centre,
spreading outward into everything around,
and then drawing life and love back into it.

Close your eyes and bring your mind and body into stillness.
Try to locate this central point of your own being.
Perhaps you can feel a creative energy,
a source of love deep within yourself too.

Homely Love

Julian shares with us these words spoken to her by God. The message is also meant for us.
Recite the words aloud.

See, I am God.
See, I am in all things.
See, I do all things.
See, I never lift my hands from my works,
nor never shall, without end.
See, I lead all things to the fulfilment I ordained for it
without beginning
by the same might, wisdom and love that I made it.
How then should anything be amiss? (11)

FOR FURTHER REFLECTION

To whom can you compare God? What image can you contrive of him? The craftsman casts an idol, a goldsmith overlays it with gold and casts silver chains for it. Someone too poor to afford a sacrifice chooses a piece of wood that will rot; he then seeks out a skilled craftsman to set up an idol that will not totter. Did you not know, had you not heard? Was it not told you from the beginning? Have you not understood how the earth was set on its foundations? He who sits enthroned above the circle of the earth, the inhabitants of which are like grasshoppers, stretches out the heavens like a cloth, spreads them out like a tent to live in.

Isaiah 40. 18–22

PRAYER

The Needlepoint Litany

For there is no doer but he. (11)

When plans haven't worked, help me know,
There is no maker but you/ There is no doer but thee.

When there's too much to do, help me know,
There is no maker but you.

When I don't understand, help me know,
There is no maker but you.

When I cannot accept, help me know,
There is no maker but you.

When I trust in luck, help me know,
There is no maker but you.

When I'm taken by surprise, help me know,
There is no maker but you.

When risks make me scared, help me know,
There is no maker but you.

When disorder reigns, help me know,
There is no maker but you.

When suffering seems pointless, help me know,
There is no maker but you.

When the past catches up, help me know,
There is no maker but you.

Homely Love

When I'm afraid of tomorrow, help me know,
There is no maker but you.

When I'm blessed, when I'm loved, help me know,
There is no maker but you.

ENDINGS

Lord,

There are many things in life
that do not seem fair,
that cause distress,
that seem to have gone wrong somewhere.
But I know that you are the source of all that exists
and that you do not let go
of what you have brought into being.

I am blind to the possibilities
within your loving plan for creation,
but I believe that everything will turn out for good,
however hopeless it may seem to my eyes.

I trust you
and I will try to respect all that you have made,
including myself and my past.
Help me not to resist your creative hand
but to let you work in my life and in others.
Give me a feeling of relief and enjoyment
in letting go and 'being' in you.

Amen.

7

Three Medicines

Healed by God

We see ourselves so foul. (40)

FROM JULIAN'S WRITINGS

Sin is the sharpest scourge that any chosen soul may be smitten with. This scourge beats up man and woman completely and makes him hateful in his own sight so that it is not long before he thinks himself worthy only to sink into hell ... Our Lord holds onto us as very precious when it seems to us that we are almost forsaken and cast away for our sin and that we have deserved it ...

By contrition we are made clean, by compassion we are made ready, & by true longing for God we are made worthy ...

for these are the medicines that every soul needs to be healed. Though healed, his wounds are seen by God, not as wounds but as trophies ... And so shall shame be turned to honour and greater joy. (39)

Julian, from the window of her anchorhold, must often have acted as a counsellor and spiritual guide. She must have gained considerable insight into human nature as she listened to the troubled stories of passers-by. Just as we find today, people were often more weighed down by their own inner struggle than by the burdens placed on them by other people.

Medieval churches were often decorated with larger-than-life wall paintings of devils tormenting guilty souls; there might be scenes of Christ enthroned, separating saints from sinners on the Day of Judgement. The Church, as today, conveyed Christ's teachings about God's love and forgiveness but hell fire was an ever-present fear. This was convenient for the authorities of the day for it encouraged poor people to wait patiently for their eternal reward in heaven and not to challenge the way things were. The suddenness of war, famine and disease, for reasons not always understood, must have reinforced in people's minds the idea that God was angry and vengeful.

Considering the times she lived in, Julian's attitude to guilt and sin is refreshing. She does not judge sinners or frighten them with warnings of dire punishments to come. Instead, she understood how much we suffer already in this lifetime from the effects of sin. We are tormented by sorrow, shame, sickness, temptation, and the finger pointing and spite of other people. The worst of all is loss of self-worth. When we beat ourselves up, as she puts it, we can be a harsher judge than God in the way we utterly condemn ourselves. God is not like the inner judge. He sees how sin brings us pain. It does not stop him loving us. On the contrary, he sees our every trouble as a war-wound to bear with pride. How can sins become a source of honour? Because, says Julian, sickness, shame, criticism and self-hatred can bring us to our knees. The acknowledgement of our wrongs, which leads us to confession, penance and reconciliation, 'is one meekness that much pleases God' (chapter 39).

Like Julian, who lay on her sickbed with the crucifix held up to her eyes, we have our Redeemer ever before us. And for those who are sick with sin, Julian prescribes three medicines: sorrow for what we have done and the desire to change; compassion for the others involved; and longing for God. These cleanse our wounds, heal the bitterness and self-hatred, and make us whole and holy. God wants us to be well, to be 'glad and merry in love' (chapter 38), says Julian, enjoying life and feeling secure in our salvation. God tells us, she says, 'Enjoy me!' Our sins are forgiven.

It is interesting that, prior to her own illness, Julian had prayed for three wounds: contrition, compassion and longing for God. When she received her revelations, Julian began to talk of them, not as wounds, but as medicines for wounds. For wounds are often already there, if only we knew it. We do not need to pray for them. Instead we might pray for that degree of self-knowledge that reveals to us what our woundedness consists of . . . and ask for healing.

SHARING JULIAN'S EXPERIENCE

Place three medicines in front of you,
taking care to leave them out of reach of children.
These can represent the three spiritual medicines Julian
   prescribes.

The first medicine is contrition.
   This is a really honest look at ourselves, 'nakedly and
   truly'.
   There may be a desire to change.
   Pray that the Holy Spirit will, as Julian puts it,
   touch you 'and begin to heal wounds'.

The second medicine is compassion.
   We can look at how our behaviour has affected others
   and how their behaviour has affected us.

Homely Love

Look lovingly at what lies behind our actions.
Pray that things will be better and different for them
and for us.

The third medicine is a longing for God
– a longing for peace, for deep contentment,
for love, for a sense of belonging,
for he 'is ground of all our whole life in love' (chapter 39).
This needs time for stillness and for 'just being'.

You might read God's response to Julian:

Behold and see.
Here you have the makings of meekness.
Here you have the makings of love.
Here you have the makings of selflessness.
Here you have the makings for enjoying me!
And, since I love you, enjoy it!
For of all the things you could do, that is what could most please me. (36)

FOR FURTHER REFLECTION

Have mercy on me, O God, in your faithful love,
in your great tenderness wipe away my offences;
wash me clean from my guilt,
purify me from my sin.

For I am well aware of my offences,
my sin is constantly in mind.
Against you, you alone, I have sinned,
I have done what you see to be wrong.

Three Medicines

But you delight in sincerity of heart,
and in secret you teach me wisdom.
Purify me with hyssop till I am clean,
wash me till I am whiter than snow.

Give me back the joy of your salvation,
sustain in me a generous spirit.
I shall teach the wicked your paths,
and sinners will return to you.

Psalm 51. 1–4, 6–7, 12–13

PRAYER

I keep you securely. (37, 40)

A modern translation of this phrase might be 'You hold
me close'. *You might prefer to use this instead of Julian's
words.*

You keep me securely   when I am criticized
You keep me securely   when I feel inadequate
You keep me securely   when I hurt other people
You keep me securely   when I am ashamed
You keep me securely   when I am embarrassed
You keep me securely   when I am laughed at
You keep me securely   when I am tempted
You keep me securely   when I feel rejected
You keep me securely   when I judge myself
You keep me securely   when I feel worthless

You keep me securely   [. . . add your own]

You keep me securely in your love.

ENDINGS

Tenderly our Lord God touches us
and blissfully clasps us,
saying to our soul,
Listen to me.
I am enough for you.
Enjoy your Saviour and your salvation. (36)

Lord,

You are enough for me.

Amen.

8

The Raindrops

Precious to God

Now is all my bitter pain and all my hard labour turned to endless joy and bliss for me and for you. (24)

FROM JULIAN'S WRITINGS

God, out of the tender love he has for us, made waters plenteous on the earth for our use and bodily comfort. But yet he likes it better that we make the same homely use of his blessed blood to wash us from our sin ... The dear worthy blood of Our Lord Jesus Christ is truly most plenteous as it is truly most precious ... Look and see: the precious plenty of his dear worthy blood descended down into hell and burst its banks and delivered all who were there who belonged to the kingdom of Heaven. The precious plenty of his dear worthy blood overflows all the earth and is ready to wash from sin all creatures of goodwill who have been and who shall be. The precious plenty of his dear worthy blood ascended up ... and evermore it flows through all the heavens, rejoicing in the salvation of all mankind.

The abundance of it is like drops of water that fall from the eaves after a great shower of rain, falling so thick that no one may number them. (12, 7)

East Anglia is a flat and sometimes water-logged place. Julian would have known plenty of water – rain, river and streams, damp walls, mud underfoot, and, at times, flooding. Her anchorhold was close to the river Wensum which ran past the bottom of St Julian's Alley.

Unpleasant though its abundance can be at times, she knew how much people depend upon water for life: fish was an important part of the medieval diet, and, as well as supplying food, water was also vital for drinking, cooking, watering crops, washing and travelling distances. It was upon the sea and river that Norwich depended for its prosperous trade. Julian might well have called water the 'precious plenty' of life.

But not everywhere in the world has water in abundance. Things that are precious to us are often the things that are not easy to come by. Precious possessions or precious loved ones often create more anxiety for us than joy because we are so afraid that we might lose them.

This is what is so wonderful about the precious plenty of Christ's blood, which washes us clean and returns us to wholeness. It is both infinitely precious and always there for us. The First Revelation of Julian which she describes in chapter 7 was of this blood of Jesus, which she saw with her own eyes in the vision rolling down from the crown of thorns. In searching for a way to describe it, she gives the homely comparison of rain pouring from the eaves of a thatched roof after a heavy shower, spreading out like a herring's scales. We are left in no doubt that there is enough for us now and in all the earthly experiences to come.

In view of the human race's apparently infinite capacity for sin and evil, there *are* times when we are tempted to doubt that there is enough forgiveness and healing and compassion in the heart of God. But in chapter 12 she makes it clear that there is nowhere and no one beyond its limit. Wherever in our lives we feel ourselves to be beyond the saving reach of God, whether in a place of unrelenting torment or trapped in the everyday grind or fearfully anticipating the future, it is as if that blood soaks down, flows around or rises up to overtake us. Julian lived a long time before the circulation of blood was understood, but her poetic description sounds almost like a circulatory system extending from time to eternity in which we are all encompassed in the ever-flowing love of God in Christ.

Outpoured blood seems a terrible and frightening thing. The description is enough to make some of us shudder. Yet in chapter 24 Julian describes Our Lord looking into his wounded side 'with a glad cheer' as he saw his precious blood all flowing out for love. Julian felt that Jesus addressed her as 'My darling' and that he was saying, 'See what delight and bliss I have in your salvation . . . enjoy it now with me.' Throughout this chapter is a recurring phrase: 'See how I loved you.' God said it to Julian; he is saying it to us.

SHARING JULIAN'S EXPERIENCE

Find something that is very precious to you,
an object such as a wedding ring
  or a photograph
  or an antique
  or a child's drawing.

It may be precious because it is worth a lot of money
  or because it cannot be replaced;
  or because it has associations.

Place it before you.
Try to put into words what it is that makes it precious to
    you.
What are your feelings as you express that?

What else is precious in your life?
Think, for example, about your health,
    your abilities,
    your family.

Finally, turn your thoughts to what God holds dear
                                    – his beloved Son Jesus.
You too are infinitely precious to him.

In Julian's Tenth Revelation, Christ showed her his
wounded side and pierced heart and said to her,

See *how* I *loveð you.* (24)

Imagine Jesus saying those words to you.

FOR FURTHER REFLECTION

And if you address as Father him who judges without
favouritism according to each individual's deeds, live out
the time of your exile here in reverent awe. For you know
that the price of your ransom from the futile way of life
handed down from your ancestors was paid, not in anything perishable like silver or gold, but in precious blood
as of a blameless and spotless lamb, Christ.

1 Peter 1. 17–19

PRAYER

The Tenth Revelation Prayer

See *how* I *loved you*. (24)

In the Julian's Tenth Revelation, Jesus tells her the ways in which he has shown her his love.
They are listed in this prayer.
As you recall the blessings of your personal life, you can add some of your own.

See *how you loved me* . . . for you gave me life
See *how you loved me* . . . for you bring me joy that will last forever
See *how you loved me* . . . for your delight is to save me
See *how you loved me* . . . for you want me to rejoice in knowing it
See *how you loved me* . . . for you died for me
See *how you loved me* . . . for you willingly suffered for me
See *how you loved me* . . . for it turned into endless joy for both of us
See *how you loved me* . . . for you long to grant all that I ask
See *how you loved me* . . . for you desire my holiness
See *how you loved me* . . . for you want me to be with you for eternity

See *how you loved me* . . .

ENDINGS

Jesus,
The precious plenty of your blood
soaks down to each hell of my own making.
Burst open captivity
and free me.

Jesus,
The precious plenty of your blood
floods over each day of my earthly living.
Wash clean its shames,
revive me.

Jesus,
The precious plenty of your blood
surges up through the future of my becoming.
Fulfil your dream in me
and bless me.

Amen.

9

The Secret

Assured by God

This is the great deed . . . hid in his blessed breast. (32)

There is a deed which the blessed Trinity shall do at the Last Day, as I see it, and when the deed shall be and how it shall be done is unknown to all creatures under Christ, and shall be until it is done. And he wills that we know because he wants us to be the more at ease in our soul and at peace in our love, relinquishing our gaze on all the tempests that might prevent us truly enjoying him. This is the great deed ordained by God from before time, treasured and hidden in his blessed breast, only known to himself, by which deed he shall make all things well. For just as the blessed Trinity made all things from nothing, so the same blessed Trinity shall make well all that is not well. (32)

Worrying. It sometimes runs through our life like a thread. It is what our mind may focus on; it can keep us awake at night; it can stop us enjoying living. Julian seems to understand this fixed gaze of the anxious mind. Some petty worries we may be ashamed even to admit to others for fear they might scoff. For ourselves, however, such anxieties can be paralysing and leave us feeling inadequate and alone. Julian assures us that God takes heed of all things, however little, low or simple. We can let God be involved in our small embarrassments. 'He wants us to know that the least thing shall not be forgotten' (chapter 32)

If little worries occupy our thoughts, then more serious concerns can overwhelm us. There are, Julian said, 'evil deeds done in our sight and so great harms caused that it seems impossible for it ever to come to a good end' (chapter 32). Injustices, addictions, losses and our own sins can cause depression and a sense of hopelessness. In chapter 27 Julian grumbles that, if it were not for sin, we wouldn't be in this state and left longing for God. 'Why by the great foreseeing wisdom of God did he not stop sin as soon as it started? For then, thought me, all should be a-well!' Julian agonizes over this issue of sin but comes to no conclusion other than that sin is somehow necessary to enable us to know ourselves and to cling to God's mercy and forgiveness. For God promises that, 'I may make all things well, I can make all things well, and I will make all things well, and you shall see yourself that all manner of things shall be well' (chapter 31).

Meanwhile our own shortcomings and those of others can absorb us. 'Upon this we look, sorrowing and mourning because of it, so that we cannot rest ourselves in the blissful beholding of God as we should do.' It is as if our gaze fixes on what causes us distress and we cannot look away and embrace happiness. But how *can* we 'leave go the beholding of all the tempests that prevent us from truly enjoying him'? How *can* we live trustingly? After all, trust is to behave as if you know someone will do what he says he will do . . . and you can never be sure.

But you can know enough about a person to feel complete assurance that they mean to do it if it is within their capability. Does God fit into that category? Yes, God's loving intention was revealed to Julian. And all around us is evidence of his power: he 'made all things out of nothing'. God's assurance to Julian was that 'That which is impossible to thee is not impossible to me. I shall keep my word in all things and I shall make all things well' (chapter 32).

How this shall come about is treasured away in the heart of God. It is God's 'privitye', his secret. What we do know is that we can gently lay aside our worries – worries about the little things, the serious things, things that are shameful, things that are impossible to put right, or so we think – and trust that God really will 'make all things well'. It is a phrase Julian repeats over and over again. She really means us to remember it, believe it, live our lives accordingly . . . and dare to be happy.

SHARING JULIAN'S EXPERIENCE

Break a piece of old crockery into fragments,
preferably something already chipped or broken.
Throw away a piece or two so that it is beyond mending.

As a focus for prayer, place the pieces around a crucifix
and sit with it for a while.

Call to mind anything personal to you
that has been damaged, wasted or lost, such as
    a relationship,
    a life,
    a career,
    a reputation,
    health,
    something you may feel was your fault.

Homely Love

You may want to ask forgiveness
or to extend forgiveness.

Look upon the crucifix as a pledge of hope.

Recall the words Jesus spoke to Julian:

> 'That which is impossible to thee
> is not impossible to me.
> I shall keep my word in all things
> and I shall make all things well.' (32)

Ask God: 'Am I the means you have chosen
for making well something that is not well?'

FOR FURTHER REFLECTION

Look at the birds in the sky. They do not sow or reap or
gather into barns; yet your heavenly Father feeds them.
Are you not worth much more than they are? Can any
of you, however much you worry, add one single cubit to
your span of life? And why worry about clothing? Think
of the flowers growing in the fields; they never have to
work or spin; yet I assure you that not even Solomon in
all his royal robes was clothed like one of these. Now if
that is how God clothes the wild flowers growing in the
field which are there today and thrown into the furnace
tomorrow, will he not much more look after you, you
who have so little faith? So do not worry; do not say,
'What are we to eat? What are we to drink? What are we
to wear?' It is the gentiles who set their hearts on all these
things. Your heavenly father knows you need them all.

Matthew 6. 26–32

The Secret

PRAYER

Bring before God the things that are 'not well'.

The following phrase from Julian's Thirteenth Revelation can be sung as a refrain between prayers of petition:

All shall be well, all man-ner of things,
all shall be well, you will see...

ENDINGS

Lord,

I believe that you care about great and noble things;
I believe that you also care about little, simple things;
I believe that you care about me.

I believe that what is impossible to me is not impossible
   to you
for I believe that you made all things from nothing.

I believe that you shall make all things well that are not
   well
and I believe that you keep your word in all things.

Homely Love

I believe that you *may* make all things well;
    I believe that you *can* make all things well;
        I believe that you *will* make all things well.

I believe that I shall see myself that

    all shall be well,

        and all shall be well,

           and all manner of things shall be well.

(using chapters 27, 31, 32)

10

Our Five Senses

Buxom to God

The nearer we be our bliss, the more we shall long. (46)

FROM JULIAN'S WRITINGS

... when the soul is stormy, troubled and left restlessly to itself, then it is time to pray to make itself supple and buxom to God ...

... we shall in our own humble daily prayers come into his presence now in this life through many intimate touchings of sweet spiritual sights and feeling, measured out to us as our simplicity may bear it ... [until,] all-possessed by God in eternity, really seeing and fully feeling him, spiritually hearing him and delightfully smelling him and sweetly swallowing him, we then shall see God face to face, homely and completely. (43)

Most of us do indeed desire God. Equally, most of us fail to live in awareness of God's presence, which leaves us feeling spiritually dry in our prayer life. It is at times like this that people turn to 'experts' and ask them how to pray. Julian's advice to those who turned to her for help, was, firstly, not to give up: when we least feel like praying is when we most need to. Secondly, she tells us, we must recognize that it is the Holy Spirit who prays in us and not we ourselves.

But she also gives us a very important hint about living and praying. We do not use to the full the means God has already given us to explore and enjoy all that there is. She encourages us to use *all* our senses: touch, smell, hearing, taste and sight. How often have we walked somewhere without even noticing the birds singing and the scent of shrubs around us? How often have we wolfed down a meal without really relishing its different tastes? Our inner world operates at half-throttle too. Often we rely on reasoning, speech and sight, and neglect our emotions and dreams. Often we fail to listen to or reflect upon what we experience and encounter day by day.

This is the crux of the matter. If we do not fully engage with our immediate physical world or know ourselves, how can we possibly expect to enter into the mystery of God? God is not to be found by shunning the world, but *through* the experience of our lives. Again and again, Julian extends God's invitation to 'enjoy' him. That entails entering fully into life with all its messy struggles. To unite with him in prayer, God does not require us to use powers beyond the natural capacity he has given us. But that natural capacity for sensing and reflecting needs to be exercised so that it may become, as Julian says, 'supple and buxom to God'.

What Julian intended to convey by 'buxom' was not what we imagine. Buxom in those days meant obedient and yielding. 'Buxom' nowadays has come to suggest plump, comely and cheery, and not a word you might use to describe the soul, though it seems consistent enough with the homeliness of spiritual life that Julian keeps telling us about. 'Responsive' is a good word to cover both ways of understanding 'buxom'.

'Supple' suggests sensitive and pliable. A supple body is a fit body, the joints working together with ease: a supple soul presumably has the same attributes of effortless and graceful movement in response to God. But suppleness requires exercise and regular stretching of every limb; the soul can be no exception.

It is clear from Julian's revelations that God wants us to live life to the full, both soul and body, fully engaged with living, enjoying our world, at ease with ourselves, at home with God, natural as God made us to be. 'Full glad and merry is our Lord to have our prayers', she says in chapter 41 – it doesn't sound as if he wants to give us a hard time of it!

SHARING JULIAN'S EXPERIENCE

Place a single flower in a vase.

Examine it, ponder it, explore it.
Enjoy it in every detail.
Use your senses.

Now that you have exercised your awareness,
think back on the day so far.
It has not simply been a series of activities.

How is your body today?
How has the weather been outside?
What about your mood *inside*?
Did you dream last night? Or daydream today?
What conversations have you had?
What effect have they had on you?
Where have you brushed against the 'sacred' in others
    and in the world around you?
What spiritual dimension in yourself has emerged
    today?
Have you felt fully alive, half-alive . . . or half-dead?

Homely Love

Then they told their story of what had happened on the road and how they had recognized him at the breaking of bread. They were still talking about all this when he himself stood among them and said to them, 'Peace be with you!' In a state of alarm and fright, they thought they were seeing a ghost. But he said, 'Why are you so agitated, and why are these doubts stirring in your hearts? See by my hands and my feet that it is I myself. Touch me and see for yourselves; a ghost has no flesh and bones as you can see I have.' And as he said this he showed them his hands and feet. Their joy was so great that they still could not believe it, as they were dumbfounded; so he said to them, 'Have you anything here to eat?' And they offered him a piece of grilled fish, which he took and ate before their eyes.

Luke 24. 35–43

Lord, I am not supple.
I can be rigid and inflexible,
hard to the touch.
I resist truths about myself;
I protect myself in case I am rejected;
I judge others harshly to boost my self-esteem.

Set me free from the defences I build
to keep others out.
Caress what is brittle in me

with your loving acceptance
until I am supple again.

Lord, I am not buxom.
I can be bitter and shrunken,
half-alive.
I fear my own potential;
I resent others who live life to the full;
I turn deaf ears to invitation or challenge.

Set me free from the limits I put
on my response to life.
Awaken what is dormant in me
with your creative joy
until I am buxom again.

(using chapter 43)

ENDINGS

GOD,

Open these eyes
in my looking
to see your creation

Open this mouth
in my eating
to taste your providence

Open these nostrils
in my breathing
to sense your closeness

Homely Love

Open these ears
in my listening
to hear your calling

Open these hands
in my working
to touch yours.

II

The Garden

Commissioned by God

There was a treasure in the earth which the Lord loved.
(51)

... I wondered what kind of labour it might be that the servant would do. And then I understood that he was doing the greatest labour and hardest work there is – he was a gardener: digging and earthing up, swinkin' and sweatin', turning over the soil and seeking the deepness, and watering the plants when they need it. And that by persistent hard work he would get sweet streams to run through it, and grow fine, plentiful fruits which he would ... offer very reverently before the lord ... I saw that the lord had endless life and all manner of goodness within himself except for that treasure which was in the earth – and that too came from the marvellous depths of the lord's endless love – but it was of no value to him until the servant had in this noble way dug it up and personally brought it before him. (51)

This picture of a great lord and his servant had come to Julian's mind at the time of the First Revelation and she returns to it later in her book. It seems to have taken 19 years and 9 months for her to gain a better understanding, which shows how worthwhile it is to return and to

61

reflect upon the significant moments in our spiritual lives. We have already pondered on the servant's clothing: now she explores various aspects of the relationship between the lord and servant.

In this passage Julian focuses on the labour itself. The lord is clearly understood as God himself. The servant, she says, is Jesus in his redeeming, self-giving mission: he wears old work clothes to symbolize the taking on of our flesh. But the servant also symbolizes Adam. Adam represents every human being. So you and I are God's gardeners too.

Julian knew some parts of Scripture very well. Perhaps this idea of a garden was suggested by the Book of Genesis where Adam dwelt in the Garden of Eden. Or by the resurrection story when Jesus appeared to Mary Magdalene in the Garden of Gethsemane. It would be nice to think that Julian had a little garden of her own to tend within the enclosure of her cell, partly for recreation but perhaps also to grow food. Like some monastic orders today, she may have been largely vegetarian. More likely, perhaps, she knew about gardening from her family home. At any rate, her description of gardening as the hardest and most exhausting work there is would indicate that she knew what it was like to have backache after a day with a spade! Details such as earthing up suggest first-hand knowledge of the kind of work gardening entails. 'Swinking' is an old word for toiling which has fallen out of use, but it is a wonderfully expressive description.

Julian tries to put our own labours into perspective. It is easy to feel bowed down by the burden and exhaustion of work and, in modern times, by the stress of schedules, audits and appraisals. She stretches our narrow perspective from deadlines to timelessness. Does our 'swinking and sweating' have any eternal purpose? Even if it does serve a good purpose, why should God want our collaboration in providing, nurturing, rescuing, teaching, building, caring and creating?

In answer to such questions, Julian talks of a 'treasure in the earth which the lord loves' (chapter 51). He brought this treasure into being in the first place and so it is already his, but its value to him depends on his servant's devoted processing of it in order to offer it back to him in love. God lacks nothing. So to imply a neediness in God makes no sense except in so far as, in loving us, God desires our involvement in his own divine life. His work is the work of love for creation. We are to collaborate with this work, just as Jesus did. Our particular task is to 'cultivate' each other and ourselves. For that 'treasure in the earth' is every soul. We are that treasure. We ourselves need digging and earthing up, turning over and watering in order that fine, abundant fruit can grow. Our own maturing to goodness and completeness is the worthy dish Jesus presents for God's delight. 'It is a dish which is lovely and pleasing to the lord.'

SHARING JULIAN'S EXPERIENCE

Place a trowel in front of you
and arrange some reminders of gardening,
such as a seed packet or flower pot.

Come into Julian's garden.
What kind of labour might it be that the servant should do? (51)

digging . . .   Where shall we gently explore?
                                 Maybe there are fears to
                                 acknowledge or resentments to
                                 let go of. There may be lovely
                                 memories to rediscover of past
                                 encounters with God.

earthing up . . .   Where do we need
                                 encouragement and protection?
                                 In our fragile self-confidence,
                                 perhaps, or creativity. What
                                 support or opportunity might
                                 we seek?

turning over the soil . . .   What is there that needs a
                                 fresh perspective or a bit of
                                 challenge? Is there a blinkered
                                 or complacent side to us we
                                 haven't faced up to before?

'seeking the deepness' . . . What is our deepest desire,
                                 our dream, our inner self, the
                                 potential for goodness and
                                 giftedness still to emerge?

watering the plants . . .   Are our basic needs being met?

Spend some time gardening with God.
Bring him the offering of yourself.

FOR FURTHER REFLECTION

This, then, is what I pray, kneeling before the Father,
from whom every fatherhood, in heaven or on earth,
takes its name. In the abundance of his glory may he,
through his Spirit, enable you to grow firm in power
with regard to your inner self, so that Christ may live in
your hearts through faith, and then, planted in love and

built on love, with all God's holy people you will have the strength to grasp the breadth and the length, the height and the depth; so that, knowing the love of Christ, which is beyond knowledge, you may be filled with the utter fullness of God.

Ephesians 3. 14–19

PRAYER

The Gardener's Prayer

(using chapter 51)

> There is a treasure in the earth
> and it is me.
> Help me find it.

> There is a treasure in the earth
> and none the same.
> Help me value it.

> There is a treasure in the earth
> and it is good.
> Help me nurture it.

> There is a treasure in the earth
> and it is hidden.
> Help me reveal it.

> There is a treasure in the earth
> and it is yours.
> Help me give it back to you.

Homely Love

Lord,

Bless my labour.
May it be a part in your work of love for creation.
Help me to be a gardener for others
that they may grow and blossom.
Help me to be a gardener of myself,
and not become neglected and tangled.
I offer back to you that gift of abundance
which you planted in the soil of my everyday living
with thanksgiving for your patient and tireless love.

Amen.

12

The Sea-bed

Safe in God

The tuther half (10)

One time my imagination was led down to the sea-bed, and there I saw hills and dales green with seaweed and sand, looking as though they were overgrown with moss. Then I understood: if a man or woman were underwater and saw God like that, as God is, always present with us, he would feel safe in body and soul and take no harm. More than that, he would have consolation and comfort beyond all telling, for God wants us to believe that we see him all the time even though we think that it is only a little, and by our believing he ever makes us gain more grace. For his will is to be seen and his will is to be sought; his will is that we abide in him and his will is that we trust him. (10)

Our belief in God can be fragile at times. Anxieties and fears can grip us much more powerfully. As we fret about the future, it is easy to imagine the worst. What is unknown and unseen can keep us in a state of constant gloom and cause us to struggle against God.

Julian leads us down to the water's edge. The sea looks so beautiful on the surface, but we fear what lies beneath . . . perhaps we will drown or be seized by monsters lurking hidden from view. What Julian reveals to us is quite different. She shows us the sea-bed as a soft mattress of moss and sand. She does not say more – how could she? She would not have known the underwater world. But today we know it to be even more marvellous than she imagined: a hushed and silent world of wonder where only gentle movement and considerably less effort are required of us than on land.

This passage seems to be about trusting faith. In the world of the here and now, we rely on our own sight and abilities for self-protection; we fear to be in any unfamiliar or unpredictable environment where we have to depend on our faith alone. But Julian says: if only we *knew* just how safe we were in that world beyond our senses, the world of the future, the world of the unseen. For there God holds us safe from harm: there are no terrors, simply an ever-welcoming embrace.

In chapter 30 she returns to this theme. She says that faith is more than just an acknowledgement of Christ. The kind of faith she is talking about is a real trust in Jesus for all eventualities, even for what is hidden from us. We are spared that knowledge of what is to come. 'Some creatures', says Julian, 'so busy themselves' trying to meddle in foreseeing the future. She encourages us instead simply to trust and rejoice in Jesus alone.

The imaginative plunge to the sea-bed of faith and trust arose from Julian's Second Revelation. Here she saw Christ's face as two distinct halves. One side was beautiful to look at. The other half was discoloured by bruising and dried blood, unrecognizable and hideous. To see Christ as 'the fairest of heaven' was how Julian expected to encounter him. She recoiled from the 'tuther half', as she called it. But as one side cleared, the other side became disfigured.

The Sea-bed

She was forced to accept that both were equally Christ. Julian is like us all. We do not want to face the hideous side of life. We avoid looking at the uglier side of ourselves; we hold back anxiously from difficulties we think may lie ahead.

But whenever our own capacity reaches its limit, God carries us and keeps us from harm. Where we expect to drown in life's cares and be swallowed by unseen monsters in the deeps, we find ourselves cushioned safely in the tender love of God's holding. We have only to believe it. God wants us to 'see' him by faith and Julian gives us some advice to help us in that. Do not give up, she says, or be grouchy, resigned to unhappiness as if it were God's will for us: instead, trust him wholeheartedly and rejoice. Then we will know 'consolation and comfort beyond all telling'.

SHARING JULIAN'S EXPERIENCE

Find a large bowl and fill it with water.
Place some pebbles and sand in the bottom.

The sand may need to be rinsed several times
before the water remains clear.

What 'lurks below the surface' in your life?
    fears for your health?
    a separation to face?
    whether you can match up to people's expectations?
    money worries?

Look into the water.
What is it actually like in the 'unseen depths'?

Homely Love

Close your eyes and imagine yourself floating gently.
Let go.

Believe yourself to be safe
in the unseen dimension of God's tender holding.

FOR FURTHER REFLECTION

And now, thus says Yahweh, he who created you, Jacob,
who formed you, Israel: Do not be afraid, for I have re-
deemed you; I have called you by your name, you are
mine. Should you pass through the waters, I shall be with
you; or through rivers, they will not swallow you up.
Should you walk through fire, you will not suffer, and
the flame will not burn you. For I am Yahweh, your God,
the Holy One of Israel, your Saviour.

Isaiah 43. 1–3

PRAYER

(using chapter 10)

Life is a continual seeking.
I'd like to think I was seeking you, Lord,
but more often it's a search for security.
I step forward gladly
when I feel firmness beneath my feet,
but those times are few.

The Sea-bed

Help me, Lord, to let go and float
into an unseen future,
happy to be and not to know,
trusting that you are there with me.
Help me, Lord, to endure,
cheerfully waiting in love.
Help me, Lord, to see you
with eyes of faith.

For though I keep on searching, you are already found.
For though I keep on doubting, I am already safe.

ENDINGS

The 'Tuther Half' Prayer

(using chapter 30)

Lord,

For what is open and clear to us,
we give thanks
and receive with reverence and meekness.

For what is hidden and spared from us,
we trust for all things and rejoice
in Our Blessed Saviour Jesus.

Amen.

The ' Tuther Half ' Prayer

For what is open to us, we give thanks and receive with reverence. For what is hidden from us, we trust in Our Saviour Jesus alone.

13

The Candleflame

Illumined by God

In light is our eternal nature. (83)

Our faith is a light, coming naturally from our endless Day, that is, God our Father; by which light our Mother Christ and our good Lord the Holy Spirit lead us in this passing life. This light is measured to us each one, there for us as we need it in the night. The light is the source of our life; the night the cause of our pain and of all our woe . . . we by his mercy and grace can make up our minds to trust our light, stepping forward in it with wisdom and strength. And at the end of suffering, suddenly our eyes shall be opened, and in the clearness of light we shall see things as they are. This light is God our Maker and the Holy Spirit in Christ Jesus our Saviour. So I saw and understood that our faith is our light in our night and the light is God our endless Day. (83)

Most of us do not know real darkness. When daylight fades, the flick of a switch floods us with light; streets are generally lit up; even in a power cut we have torches and matches to hand. In Julian's time a winter's night could be dark indeed. The poor did not have beeswax candles: rush lights or firelight cast only the dimmest glow. There were no spectacles or corrective surgery to help their ailing eyesight. To a medieval woman, being able to see was not something she took for granted.

In chapter 52 Julian likens our human condition of 'woe and tribulation' to a kind of blindness: we fumble through our lives, guessing, knocking against things, frustrated, clumsy, frightened and lost. And yet our 'eternal nature' is light, and in light we are transformed and freed. Julian says we are a 'muddle so marvellous' of good and bad, light and darkness.

So what is Julian's spiritual meaning when she talks of light? Light, she says in chapter 84, is love. And the light of love is threefold: it is a love for God himself, a love for ourselves as God's creation, and love for all that God loves. This is the light measured out to us to keep us going in this life: the gift of love. For by love we gain true understanding. We start to see things as they really are, without distortions or shadows or obstacles to view. Light and love become the same thing when love opens our eyes. Some days we are very blind. At other times our eyes are suddenly opened. And the eyes Julian is talking about are not the eyes in our head but the eyes of our heart.

Enlightenment is to shed light on a situation or person so that we can see more than the partial view we had before. How often we say, 'It had never occurred to me that . . .' or, 'Sorry, I hadn't realized . . .' So, under what circumstances do we come to realize the many-sidedness of a situation or see more to a person than we saw before? It is when we look lovingly. When we take time rather than make hasty judgements; when we really listen to what people are saying; when we are open enough to change our mind; when we are humble, for we do not always need to be in the right or to know best, unless, that is, we have a poor sense of our own self-worth.

This is where the love of God, the love of self and the love of others are all important. For love of God gives us a desire for justice and truth that urges us to look beyond what is in front of our noses. Love of self is a regard for our best, our deepest self, that dignity and integrity and self-respect which is not dependent on getting our own way or putting other people down or grasping for affection and status. The security of knowing how lovable and precious we are enables us to stand back or stand up for ourselves or stand firm or let go or say sorry or admit to a change of mind when something inside tells us what is right. Love of others leads us to believe in them, to give them second chances, to challenge, to take risks in trusting, to respect their differences and uniqueness, to see through their eyes. This kind of love is not so much a warm feeling as an open attitude. Open heart and open eyes – the light of love.

SHARING JULIAN'S EXPERIENCE

Sit for a while in a darkened room.
Light some candles.
They will reveal what you could not make out before.

When you are calmed and at peace,
think of a situation which has bothered you recently.
How have you viewed it up to now?
Ask God for the light of love so that you can see more
    clearly.

Homely Love

The light of love, says Julian, is a threefold gift:

Love of God,
>the desire to recognize where truth and right and goodness lie.

Love of yourself,
>so that you can see what is truly best for you,
>so that you can voice your own needs.

Love of others,
>so that you can understand things from their perspective,
>so that you can acknowledge their needs and interests too.

FOR FURTHER REFLECTION

>This is what we have heard from him and are declaring to you: God is light, and there is no darkness in him at all. If we say that we share in God's life while we are living in darkness, we are lying, because we are not living the truth. But if we live in light, as he is in light, we have a share in one another's life, and the blood of Jesus, his Son, cleanses us from all sin.

>*1 John 1. 5–7*

The Candleflame

The Twelfth Revelation: 'I it am' (26)

This means 'I am He' in modern English.
In the Twelfth Revelation Christ speaks words of strength
and comfort to Julian.
They are reproduced here as a response to a modern prayer
for enlightenment.

The prayer and the response can be used separately
or else using two voices in dialogue as below:

I don't know what happiness is any more.	I am He.
I cannot see it when it stares me in the face.	I am He.
I've lost all sense of purpose in my life.	It is I you are looking for.
There's little feeling left.	It is I you love.
I'm restless and I don't know why.	It is I you are drawn to.
I work and struggle, but what for?	It is I you serve.
What would fill my emptiness?	It is I you long for.
What do I really want?	It is I you desire.
Who has the answer?	It is I, your meaning.
My life is 'in bits' as they say.	It is I who am all.
I doubt even what I used to believe.	It is I Holy Church teaches.
Will I ever find what I'm searching for?	It is I here with you now.

Homely Love

And after this Our Lord showed himself in more glory than it seemed I had seen him before, and I learned from this that our soul shall never have rest until it comes to him, knowing that he is fullness of joy, homely and respectful, full of happiness and life. Our Lord Jesus often said, 'It is I . . .' (26)

Jesus,

My soul shall never find its rest
until it comes to you.
I know that you are my fulfilment,
my deepest joy.
I can come home to you,
find my dignity in you,
be happy in you.
In you I can take hold of life itself.

You stand glorious before me.
You reveal yourself as you are
and say to me, 'It is I whom you love.'
Help me to stand before you,
to dare to reveal myself
in my poverty to you.
Help me to come just as *I* am
and say to you,
'It is I . . .
the one you love.'

14

Motherhood

Nurtured by God

He feeds us with himself. (60)

FROM JULIAN'S WRITINGS

And in our spiritual birthing, he shows tenderness of care beyond any other mother in so much as our soul is of more value in his eyes. He kindles our understanding, he directs our ways, he eases our consciences, he comforts our soul, he lightens our heart and gives us, in part, knowledge and love of his blessed Godhead . . . If we fall, hastily he picks us up in his lovely embrace and touches us graciously . . . A mother may allow her child to fall sometimes and feel distress in various ways to be a lesson, but she will never, out of love, allow any kind of danger to come to her child. And though it is possible for our earthly mother to allow her child to perish, our heavenly mother Jesus will not allow us who are his children to die. (61)

Reading this passage, you might be forgiven for thinking that Julian had made a mistake in calling Jesus 'our mother'. But she spends chapters 57–64 exploring this subject of the true motherhood of Christ, so it was no slip of the pen.

It sounds as though Julian's own experience of mothering was a good one. We know that her mother was there in her illness. It is possible that she had been a mother her-

self. In every reference to motherhood, she speaks affection-
ately. She speaks often of Holy Church as our mother and
of Mary, the mother of Our Saviour. In her near-fatal
experience of 1373, Julian, like Jesus, has her mother with
her at her death as well as at her birth.

For some of us, motherhood can be a touchy subject.
Mothers can often get things very wrong. But Jesus is the
ideal mother. He understands the needs of his child and
allows the relationship to change as the child grows up.
He gives his children freedom to learn by their mistakes,
though he is always there to support them if they fall and to
watch that they come to no harm. Julian says that we need
to fall, in order to grow to understand the limits of our own
strength and the extent of God's love for us. 'He wants all
our love fastened on him', but he does not bind us to him by
any sense of obligation or guilt. His is the kind of love that
lets his children be and become themselves.

We may doubt at first whether the image of Jesus as
mother is helpful. But it becomes clearer as Julian explores
the role of motherhood. A mother gives teaching and moral
guidance by spending time with her children and involving
them in her own good works. She nourishes them when
they are hungry; rescues them when they fall over; nurses
them when they are sick and comforts them when they are
distressed. As adults we continue to need these things. Jesus
provides them. 'He kindles our understanding, he directs
our ways.' By involving us in his own mission, 'he makes
us love all that he loves'. 'He feeds us with himself . . . with
the Blessed Sacrament that is the precious food of life itself.' Julian calls the Church 'our mother's breast'. When
we fall into sin, Jesus gives his own life, for 'It is his job to
save us.' He heals us as 'a kind nurse', his hands 'ready and
diligently about us'. And like a wise mother he will exercise

tough love: 'if he sees that it be more profit to us to mourn and to weep, he allows it with sorrow and pity for the appropriate time out of love.'

But we need to allow Jesus to be a true mother to us. That requires us to be child-like. It is not the same as childish. Julian is not encouraging us to be immature, self-willed, cowering or rebellious. She is talking about the attributes of a natural child – wondering, trusting, creative and spontaneously loving. She does not say that we are to be anything less than adults in our everyday relations. Indeed, since the whole book is about God's love for us, then we have no need to tiptoe submissively round each other nor to dominate others to make ourselves feel more important. We can be mature adults while child-like before God, and

brought again by the motherhood of mercy and grace into the natural condition in which we were made.

SHARING JULIAN'S EXPERIENCE

Make a hot drink for yourself,
a mugful of something relaxing.
Sip it very slowly.
It would be a good bedtime exercise.

This is an opportunity to give yourself some mothering.
Jesus is with you.

Tell him all about the day.
What were you pleased with?
What are you grateful for?
What didn't go well?

Remind yourself what you learned.
Ask the questions that you need to ask.

In what areas do you need to say a loving but firm 'No!'
to yourself?

Do you have the capacity to hear him say, 'I love you?'
. . . or to say it to yourself?

FOR FURTHER REFLECTION

When Israel was a child I loved him, and called my son
out of Egypt. But the more I called, the further they went
away from me; they offered sacrifice to Baal and burnt
incense to idols. I myself taught Ephraim to walk, I myself took them by the arm, but they did not know that
I was the one caring for them, that I was leading them
with human ties, with leading strings of love, that, with
them, I was like someone lifting an infant to his cheek,
and that I bent down to feed him.

Hosea 11. 1–4

PRAYER

Great God, Almighty, life itself,
you knew and loved us before time began.

Out of your deep, deep love and knowing,
by the endless foreseeing wisdom of the Trinity,
sprang your desire that Jesus be
    our Mother,
    our Brother,
    our Saviour.

True Father, who wills;
True Mother, who works;
Good Lord, Holy Spirit, who strengthens;
O God, source of being,
our part is to love you.

Father of all,
accept our reverence, our thanks, our praise;
Mother of all,
have mercy and pity on us;
Spirit of life,
give us your help and grace. (59)

Amen.

ENDINGS
(from chapter 59 adapted)

It is You:

> the might and goodness of Fatherhood;
> the wisdom of Motherhood;
> the light and grace that is all-blessed Love.

It is You:

> the Trinity;
> the Unity;
> the sovereign goodness of all things.

It is You:

> the love in me;
> the longing in me;
> the endless fulfilment of all true desires.

15

The Glowing Tile

Reminded by God

My eye I set on the cross. (69)

FROM JULIAN'S WRITINGS

And as I soon as I began to sleep I thought the Fiend had me by the throat, sticking his face, like a young man's face, right into mine. And it was long and amazingly thin, I never saw one like it. Its colour glowed red like a floortile newly fired with black spots on it like black freckles, fouler than the tile. His hair was red as rust, short in front with curls at the temples. He grinned at me with a shrewd look, showing white teeth, which made him seem, I thought, all the more ugly. Neither body nor hands were shapely. With his paws he held me by the throat and would have strangled me, but he dare not. This ugly vision was while I was sleeping, unlike any of the others. And all this time I trusted to be saved and kept by the mercy of God. (66)

In the space of just five hours from 4 a.m. to 9 a.m. Julian had been blessed with 15 revelations of Christ. You would think this would be the source of her greatest pride. The truth was, she felt embarrassed about it. During the morning a thumping headache returned and she felt weak and sorry for herself. When someone asked how she was, she laughed off the visions as delirium. Like St Peter at the

84

crowing of the cock, Julian then wept with shame that it had taken so little to dismiss the presence of God in her life.

That night she fell into a troubled sleep. It was then that the devil appeared in her dreams to throttle her. Julian describes his face like a tile hot from the kiln. Glazed floor tiles, made from fired clay and often red in colour, were made in medieval times for buildings such as churches, though Julian was unlikely to have had any in her own home. I wonder if she had ever seen a local kiln when the roof of the pit was removed to reveal glowing new tiles? The intensity of its heat must have seemed like the torments of hell. If she had, it seems to have left a fearful and lasting impression. Fortunately, Julian awoke to find that this was only a nightmare – the person at her bedside was not the devil, just someone bathing her temples.

In this feverish state, tormenting herself with guilt for the way she was behaving, Julian felt pulled between the forces of goodness and evil. Yet it was in this unpeaceful state that she was blessed with her last revelation of God's love. This, the sixteenth, was a vision of the city of her soul, set restfully in the middle of her heart, and Jesus dwelling within 'in his homeliest home' (chapter 67).

We, too, lurch from spiritual heights to the depths of despair. Out of embarrassment we too can make light of our relationship with God when people ask us about it. Often sin and evil seem so much more real to us than God's presence, and lead us to doubt what we have experienced spiritually. Illness and tiredness too can distort our perception of how things really are. Guilt comes easily and we can find ourselves like Julian in the stench of self-disgust. And we all know what it is to toss and turn on the pillows at night, tormented by a worry, guilt or fear. Such horrors may well seem like a grotesquely mocking face, someone with power to see right through us and threatening to extinguish our very life. But Jesus draws us back to faith and tells us, as he told Julian, to trust in God.

As soon as Julian recalled what God had revealed to her earlier that morning – and thought about how much faith there was in the Church as a whole, however little she herself might have – she found that the horrors vanished and that peace took their place. It is good advice for us too when we are overwhelmed by guilt or fear. This is the time to turn to other believers for support and to find reassurance from memories of the way God has revealed his love for us in the past.

I set my eyes on the same Cross which had comforted me before that time. (69)

SHARING JULIAN'S EXPERIENCE

Get out your photograph albums.
Find a photograph of a happy time
or some other souvenir of
when God seemed especially present in your life.

Sit quietly with it for a while.

When Julian began to wonder if her revelations were
   real, Jesus said to her

'Now know it well, that it was no raving that you saw today:
but take it;
believe it;
hold on to it;
comfort yourself with it;
trust yourself to it;
and you shall not be overcome.' (68, 70)

So take your own memory of something good.
Reinstate its importance in your life
as a sign of God's love and care for you
then, now and in times to come . . .

    take it
    believe it
    hold on to it
    comfort yourself with it
    trust what it is saying to you.

FOR FURTHER REFLECTION

For I am certain of this: neither death nor life, nor angels, nor principalities, nothing already in existence and nothing still to come, nor any power, nor the heights nor the depths, nor any created thing whatever, will be able to come between us and the love of God, known to us in Christ Jesus our Lord.

Romans 8. 38–39

PRAYER

(using chapters 68, 70)

    I know it well.

It wasn't imagination
to recall how you blessed me then,
how you carried me then,
how you healed me.

    I know it well.

It isn't superstition
to say that you save me from disaster,
that you guide me through darkness,
that you bring me friends.

    I know it well.

It won't be pie in the sky
to believe that you will walk with me,
that you will surround me with your love,
that you will bring me life.

    I know it well.

ENDINGS

(using chapters 68, 70)

Lord,

I embrace you
I believe you
I remain in you
I comfort myself with you
I entrust myself to you

I shall not be overcome.

Amen.

16

The City Centre

Still in God

In us is his homeliest home. (67)

And then our Lord opened my spiritual eyes and showed me my soul in the midst of my heart. I saw the soul so large as if it were an endless world and as if it were a blessed kingdom; and from the conditions I saw in it, I realized it was a sight to admire. In the midst of that city sits our Lord Jesus, God-and-Man, a beautiful person and great in stature, highest bishop, solemn king, most worshipful lord; and I saw him clad in all solemnity. He sits in the soul in rightful peace and rest ... the place that Jesus takes in our soul he shall never ever remove as far I could see, for in us is his homeliest home and his endless dwelling. (67)

In Julian's day Norwich was the second largest city of England. Trade flooded in from Flanders and the Rhineland; and exports of famous Norfolk wool and worsted cloth brought wealth. There were plenty of merchants and craftsmen from the Continent to add to Norwich's own population of some 6,000 people within a walled city of a square mile. It was a bewildering mix of hovels, tanneries, warehouses, breweries, dye-houses, fish wharves and markets, together with dozens of churches, monasteries and convents. The sacred and the secular closely co-existed as if it were the most natural thing in the world. In the midst of Julian's teeming world stood the magnificent Norman cathedral, its spire being rebuilt to dominate the city skyline.

Before Julian became an anchoress on the edge of the city, her life like all those who lived in medieval Norwich would probably have been full of noise and bustle. Her ears would have been ringing from the bells of countless churches, the cries of market people, the noises of pigs and dogs and hens. Her nostrils were filled with the stench of fish and open drains and slaughterhouses, her shoes stained with the dirt of unpaved, unswept streets and alleys. As with our modern existence, peace and rest probably did not figure very prominently in Julian's life. The image of a city is a powerful symbol of the condition of our lives, for our inner selves are sometimes no less frantic and stressful than our external circumstances.

This does not mean that God is far away. Julian's Sixteenth Revelation has a powerful message for us: we don't need the quiet of a cloister or desert island for Jesus to feel right at home with us. He is with us in the stresses and strains, in the noise and rush of daily life. He is not a Sundays-only God. He is Emmanuel, meaning God-with-us, that is, Monday to Friday as well. Our busyness can sometimes lead us to doubt God's power and willingness to help us and to question whether we deserve his continued presence. It is at such moments we need reminding that Jesus feels at home in us – in fact, it is where he feels most at home. And because he reigns at the heart of our being, we can draw upon inner resources to cope with all that life brings. For all the panic and rush in our everyday living, there remains a still centre in all of us. In our prayer life we can learn to locate it.

During the long night of her revelations of Christ, Julian remained feverish, slipping in and out of consciousness. It was in this unpeaceful state that she was blessed with this last revelation of God's love, the vision of the city of her soul, set restfully in the middle of her heart, and Jesus dwelling within 'in his homeliest home' (chapter 67). 'This was a delectable sight and a restful showing', said Julian. She found the revelation profoundly reassuring. The difficulties and sufferings and frights of her illness were not removed from her, but she could take strength from the knowledge that, with God with her, she would not be lost or overwhelmed. 'You shall not be overcome', Jesus said to her. Julian repeated this,

> He did not say, 'You shall not be tossed about by tempest;
> you shall not be burdened; you shall not be stressed',
> but he said 'You shall not be overcome'. (68)

SHARING JULIAN'S EXPERIENCE

Unfold a large street map before you.
Let it symbolize the city of your soul.

In what ways are you like the city?

> Complex? . . . confused? . . . busy going nowhere?
> full of interest? . . . ever-changing? . . . industrious?
> thriving? . . . competitive? . . . traffic-jammed?

It is in you that Jesus wants to make his home.

Reverently place a lighted candle in the centre of the map.

Be still.

Try to locate the place of peace and rest deep within yourself.

You might like to say this mantra using Julian's own words.

Julian herself probably repeated it during the second night of her visions:

Jesus is at home in me
and he will never leave. (67)

FOR FURTHER REFLECTION

Then I saw a new heaven and a new earth; the first heaven and the first earth had disappeared now, and there was no longer any sea. I saw the holy city, the new Jerusalem, coming down out of heaven from God, prepared as a bride dressed for her husband. Then I heard a loud voice call from the throne, 'Look, here God lives among human beings. He will make his home among them; they will be his people, and he will be their God, God-with-them. He will wipe away all tears from their eyes; there will be no more death, and no more mourning or sadness or pain. The world of the past has gone.'

Revelation 21. 1–4

Homely Love

PRAYER

He did not say, 'You shall not be tossed about by tempest; you shall not be burdened; you shall not be stressed', but he said, 'You shall not be overcome'. (68)

You did not say I would not have tempests in my life,

    stormy relationships,
    unresolved anger,
    crises and outbursts,
    accidents and crimes,
    the suddenness of death,
    the upheavals of leaving,

but . . . you said I shall not be overcome.

You did not say I would not have burdens on my
    shoulders,

    responsibility for those I love,
    other people's expectations,
    guilt and stress,
    debts and obligations,
    work and deadlines,
    disability and illness,

but . . . you said I shall not be overcome.

The City Centre

You did not say I would not have worries on my mind,

   fears for the future,
   concerns for my family,
   fretting about security and money,
   wondering what other people think,
   terror of losing what I have,
   dread of the unknown,

but . . . you said I shall not be overcome.

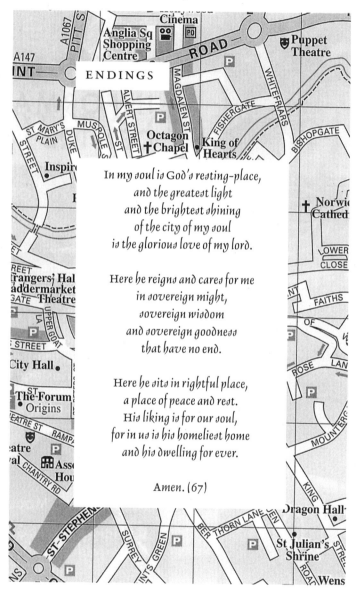

Homely Love

ENDINGS

In my soul is God's resting-place,
and the greatest light
and the brightest shining
of the city of my soul
is the glorious love of my lord.

Here he reigns and cares for me
in sovereign might,
sovereign wisdom
and sovereign goodness
that have no end.

Here he sits in rightful place,
a place of peace and rest.
His liking is for our soul,
for in us is his homeliest home
and his dwelling for ever.

Amen. (67)

An Order for Morning Prayer

For group worship, responses are printed in bold type. Here, as elsewhere, the Julian sources appear in brackets at the end of each item.

Opening Responses

> Let us flee to our Lord
> **And we shall be strengthened.**
> Let us touch him
> **And we shall be made clean.**
> Let us cling to him
> **And we shall be secure and safe**
> **from all manner of peril.** (77)

> Glory be to God the Trinity,
> our Maker and Keeper,
> our Everlasting Lover.
> **Who made all things for love**
> **and by the same love keeps it,**
> **and shall keep it without end.**
> **Amen.** (74, 8)

Homely Love

Psalm 103

(verses 1–5, 11–17)

Bless, Yahweh, my soul,
from the depths of my being, his holy name;
bless Yahweh, my soul,
never forget all his acts of kindness.

He forgives all your offences,
cures all your diseases,
he redeems your life from the abyss,
crowns you with faithful love and tenderness;
he contents you with good things all your life,
renews your youth like an eagle's.

As the height of heaven above earth,
so strong is his faithful love for those who fear him.
As the distance of east from west,
so far from us does he put our faults.

As tenderly as a father treats his children,
so Yahweh treats those who fear him;
he knows of what we are made,
he remembers that we are dust.

As for a human person – his days are like grass,
he blooms like the wild flowers;
as soon as the wind blows he is gone,
never to be seen there again.

But Yahweh's faithful love for those who fear him
is from eternity and for ever.

A 'Psalm'
using Julian of Norwich

Our faith is a light;
it comes from God our endless Day:
The light is the source of our life;
it is light in our darkness.
**We by his mercy and grace
can trust the light.**

We step forward in it
with wisdom and strength.
The light is love.
And in this love our life is everlasting.
**We by his mercy and grace
can trust the light.**

At the end of suffering,
suddenly our eyes shall be opened;
in the clearness of light
we shall see things as they are.
**We by his mercy and grace
can trust the light.**

This light is God our Maker
and the Holy Spirit
in Christ Jesus our Saviour.
**We by his mercy and grace
can trust the light.** (83, 84)

Word of God

He has let us know the mystery of his purpose, according
to his good pleasure which he determined beforehand in
Christ, for him to act upon when the times had run their
course: that he would bring everything together under
Christ, as head, everything in the heavens and everything on earth.

Ephesians 1. 9–10

Reflection

And all this he blissfully showed me as if he were saying,
'See, I am God. See, I am in all things. See, I never let
go my hands from my works, nor ever shall. See, I lead
all things to the end I ordained for it by the same might,
wisdom and love that I made it.'

Our Lord God doeth all.
There is no doer but he. (11)

A 'Canticle'

using Julian of Norwich

All shall be well, all manner of things shall be well.

Before time began,
our life has been grounded
in our true Mother Jesus.

Fair and sweet is our heavenly Mother
in the sight of our soul;
precious and lovely are his gracious children
in the sight of our heavenly Mother.

In taking our nature he quickened us;
in his dying he bore us to endless life;
He, all love, bears us to joy.

Then shall be revealed to us
the meaning of his sweet words,
'All shall be well, you shall see for yourself
that all manner of things shall be well.'

Through his own foreseeing wisdom,
and the almighty power of the Father
and the sovereign goodness of the Holy Spirit,
this new beginning shall last without end, ever to begin.

All shall be well, all manner of things shall be well.

(60, 63)

Prayers

Give us eyes to see you, Lord, in all your creation.
**For you have made all that is made and love all that you
have made.**

When we fall through our frailty or blindness,
Touch us, stir us, hold on to us.

Lead us so deeply into God that we truly come to know
ourselves.
Christ be our way

For the times we are reckless in our living or in the
keeping of our hearts,
Christ be our way

For all brought low by the sorrows and storms that
befall them,
Christ be our way

You mean your healing for all mankind: Lord, unite us
in love.
Christ be our way

We rejoice that you are our Father and so we pray:
Our Father . . .

Our Lady is Our Mother too: in Christ we are born of
her.
Mary, rejoice with us in the love of Christ.

(9, 79, 56, 36, 78, 52, 59, 55)

Concluding Prayer and Blessing

Help us to cling to you, Lord, as children to their mother.
May we understand how tenderly enfolded we are in your
loving embrace and come to trust in the goodness of your
plan for all time as Julian taught us. With her we pray,

> **God, of your goodness, give us yourself,**
> **for you are enough for us.**
> **In you alone we have everything.**
> **Amen.** (5)

> In the name of the Father, Son and Holy Spirit,
> **our Maker, our Lover and our Keeper.**
> **Amen.** (5)

An Order for Evening Prayer

For group worship, responses are printed in bold type. Here, as elsewhere, the Julian sources appear in brackets at the end of each item.

Opening Responses

To understand and know the goodness of God is our prayer.
It reaches down to the humblest level of our need.

It is the same grace that our soul seeks now
and ever shall.

And therefore by his grace and help let our spirits stand and gaze.
We for ever marvel at this love beyond all telling. (6)

Glory be to God the Trinity,
our Maker and Keeper,
our Everlasting Lover.
**Who made all things for love
and by the same love keeps it,
and shall keep it without end.
Amen.** (4, 8)

Homely Love

Psalm 4

When I call, answer me, God, upholder of my right.
In my distress you have set me at large;
take pity on me and hear my prayer!

Children of men, how long will you be heavy of heart,
why love what is vain and chase after illusions?

Know that Yahweh performs wonders for his faithful,
Yahweh listens when I call to him.

Be careful not to sin,
speak in your hearts, and on your beds keep silence.

Loyally offer sacrifices, and trust in Yahweh.

Many keep saying, 'Who will put happiness before our
    eyes?'
Let the light of your face shine on us.

Yahweh, to my heart you are a richer joy
than all their corn and new wine.

In peace I lie down and at once fall asleep,
for it is you and none other, Yahweh, who make me rest
    secure.

An Order for Evening Prayer

A 'Psalm'

using Julian of Norwich

> **God is all that is good**
> **and is the goodness of all good things.**
>
> His goodness enfolds all his creatures
> and all his blessed works.
> It is beyond measure and without end
> for he is without end.
> **God is all that is good**
> **and is the goodness of all good things.**
>
> He has made us for himself alone
> and restored us by his passion
> and keeps us in his love.
> All this is of his goodness.
> **God is all that is good**
> **and is the goodness of all good things.**
>
> He is true rest.
> God wills that we should know him.
> His pleasure is that we rest in him.
> For nothing less than him could suffice.
> **God is all that is good**
> **and is the goodness of all good things.**
>
> Bless you, O Lord,
> our Maker and Keeper, our Everlasting Lover.
> Who made all things for love
> and by the same love it is held and shall be without end.
> **God is all that is good**
> **and is the goodness of all good things.** (5, 4, 8)

Homely Love

Word of God

Let us keep our eyes fixed on Jesus, who leads us in our faith and brings it to perfection: for the sake of the joy which lay ahead of him, he endured the cross, disregarding the shame of it, and has taken his seat at the right of God's throne. Think of the way he persevered against such opposition from sinners and then you will not lose heart.

Hebrews 12. 2–3

Reflection

And with this our good Lord said, with such bliss, 'See how I loved you!' It was as if he had said, 'My darling, behold and see your Lord, your God, who is your maker and your endless joy. See what joy and bliss I have in your salvation!' And, 'For love of me, share my joy!'

All shall be brought to joy.
See how he loves us. (21, 24)

A 'Canticle'
using Julian of Norwich

God is true rest and it is his pleasure that we rest in him.

My soul is so loved by God Most High
that it is beyond earthly telling.
Nothing in creation can know
how much, how sweetly, how tenderly
our Maker loves us.

Great is the wonder
that he who is above all
should want to be at home
with humankind in our lowly state.

And so, by his grace and help,
my spirit stands and gazes,
tirelessly marvelling at this love
Almighty God has for us in his goodness.

A love so high, it is beyond compare or measure.
I shall never stop wanting nor longing
until that time when I shall enjoy him in fullness
and yearn no more. (5, 6, 7)

God is true rest and it is his pleasure that we rest in him.
(5)

Prayers

Our God in whom we have our being,
We thank you for making us.

Jesus, who took our created nature upon yourself,
We thank you for loving us.

Our Lord, Holy Spirit, whose work of love and grace
    flows out without end,
We thank you for helping and strengthening us.

When we are overwhelmed by cares, help us to realize
    the littleness of creatures.
We cling to your goodness

When we have no ease of heart or soul, help us to seek
you who are our true rest.
We cling to your goodness

Clothe, wrap, embrace, and completely enclose with
tender love all those dear to us.
We cling to your goodness

Stir us with abundant love towards our neighbours to
serve and esteem them.
We cling to your goodness

We rejoice that you are our Father and so we pray:
Our Father . . .

May the love of the sweet Mother who bore our Saviour
help us as we pray.
**So may all the blessed company of heaven whose dear
love and endless friendship we enjoy. Amen.**

(59, 5, 8, 52, 6)

Concluding Prayer and Blessing

Teach us, Lord, the lesson of love and bring us the comfort
that Julian received. May we, like her, find true peace in
knowing that our God and Lord is at home with those he
created and keeps for ever in his love.

May the power of God be our strength against all
that is evil.
Amen.

May the love of God be our everlasting joy and bliss.
Amen.

May the goodness of God come down to us in our need.
Amen. (4, 6)

In the name of the Father, Son and Holy Spirit,
our Maker, our Lover and our Keeper.
Amen. (5)

Acknowledgements and Sources

I have used the Exeter Press transcript of Julian's original text which is based on British Library Sloane Manuscript No. 2499, keeping as close as possible to the original wording but adapting it myself where necessary to make the meaning clearer. Wherever I have used or closely adapted Julian's own words in the prayers, these appear in the older font, and I have used the original as often as possible, so that the reader can feel close to Julian.

Quotations from Julian's *Showing of Love* are referred to by chapter number shown in brackets.

All biblical quotations are from the New Jerusalem Bible, published and copyright © 1966, 1967 and 1968 by Darton, Longman & Todd Ltd and Doubleday, a division of Random House, Inc. and used by permission.